T0102906

100
Shades of Life

100
Shades of Life

MANJURI NEOGI

PARTRIDGE
A Penguin Random House Company

Copyright © 2015 by Manjuri Neogi.

ISBN: Hardcover   978-1-4828-4758-1
                Softcover   978-1-4828-4759-8
                eBook   978-1-4828-4757-4

All rights reserved. No part of this book may be used or reproduced by any means, graphic, electronic, or mechanical, including photocopying, recording, taping or by any information storage retrieval system without the written permission of the publisher except in the case of brief quotations embodied in critical articles and reviews.

Because of the dynamic nature of the Internet, any web addresses or links contained in this book may have changed since publication and may no longer be valid. The views expressed in this work are solely those of the author and do not necessarily reflect the views of the publisher, and the publisher hereby disclaims any responsibility for them.

Print information available on the last page.

To order additional copies of this book, contact
Partridge India
000 800 10062 62
orders.india@partridgepublishing.com

www.partridgepublishing.com/india

For my husband Debashis and son Aryaman,
my extraordinary men in life and living.

Contents

Preface

Writing poetry came naturally to me. Born and brought up amidst the nature, I could see and feel beauty all around me. Life, nature and various shades of living always attracted me. So, I kept on penning a few lines every now and then. Over the years my collection got to a respectable size. I then thought of publishing my work of best 100 poems.

This book contains various colours of life and love. It is mainly intended to warm up the hearts of readers with the light of love. I have dealt with the pain of love as much as the pleasure of it. The journey of writing these poems was completely based on my mood at that particular moment.

All the work is that of fiction. It is not intended for anyone in particular. I hope my readers discover themselves in this collection of my verses.

Manjuri Neogi

~Manjuri~

Between Going And Gone!

How would I call you,
To walk a few steps..
With me..
On that old broken road..
Which now mosses adorn..
Whispers forgotten lorn
Of unrequited love..
Cloud laden sky..
Twilight closes eyes..
November half the way..
You stranded, me lost..
And clasped hands freezes..
Autumn wants to leave..
Winter says no..
We.. standing on two sides..
Divided by pride..

We come and go..
Sometimes like sound..
Mostly like echo..
But still its true..
That you stay..
In some heart's bent..
You, your scent..
You cross my eyes..
Each time I see the world..
I wonder, how shall I live..
If you stop giving me pain..
Never stop... go on..
Promise you got to make..
That pain you shall give..
In them I live..
In that broken, forlorn street..
With, water.. fallen leaf and some wind!

Rekindle!

Hold my tired soul for a while,
Blow some air into it..
Long since I lived a little..
Strangulated in life's pit!

Catch my eyes, put into yours..
Long since I saw..
Frozen vision awaits you..
My Tears Await a Thaw!

Clasp my fingers with yours..
They have fallen still..
Words of heart, reach them not..
How will you heal?

Take me to your chest once..
Let your heart thrive..
Sound that shall reach my ears..
Shall keep me alive!

Rekindle the fire within you,
And let the flames burn..
Either I emerge anew from it..
Or into ashes, I turn!

Unreasonable Love!

My love for you knows no reason..
No limits is it aware of..

I love you, like the floating cloud..
Clouds that love its sky..
I love you like the flowing river..
River that loves its ocean..
I love you like the singing bird..
Bird that love its branches..
I love you like a butterfly..
A butterfly that love is flower..
I love you like the moon and stars..
Planets that love the night sky..
I love you like a drop of dew..
Dew that love its winter grass..

I too don't know how and why..
I love you so very much!

Drunken With Life

At this moment all is beautiful..
Yes I am drunk..
Life served me wine, I drank..
Now its time, I slip into you..
My words are more drunk..
My poetry dresses in trance..
Come my love, come to me..
Hold my hand... let us dance..
You gave me joy infinite..
In two days you gave me a world..
They say Drunkards do not lie..
Then am too is telling the truth...
However momentary those hours were..
They came.. and went by..
None saw... but you and me..
Look within... in you I still lie..
You fed me with poison...
I got my life...
I breathe in you.. I live in you...
Especially in moments like these..

When I forget myself...
Ego dissolves...
And I just mix in you...
Come before tomorrow...
Before my senses are back..
With senses I too act, like you..
Uncaring, unloving, I become!
Come now, night is young...
Younger in my love...
In you I once emerged..
In you... let me end...
Today, tomorrow and always!

Journey Towards Oblivion!

I want to speak to you..
In a language alien..
Neither you understand..
What I say..
Nor I grasp.. what I blabber...
Let words die..
Within our conversation!
I want to dream of you..
In a reverie unknown..
Neither you appear..
In it fully..
Nor I let you go..
Even partially..
I want to walk with you..
Though the path untrodden..
Neither you know..
Where it leads to...
Nor am I aware..
Of its final goal..

Come let the dream begin..
Of undeciphered words..
Walking towards unknown..
Blindfolded.. life's eye..
Neither life sees us..
Nor we see life...
But we run... together..
To reach somewhere...
Someday...
Where celestial joy..
Bedecks our path..
We tip and fall...
Onto each other..
We rise again...
With each other...
And colours burst out..
Into a rainbow...
Before we fade into oblivion!

Evening!

Evening arrives on my senses..
Am getting engulfed..
My breath tangled..
My pulse ticking...
As I run down the corridor..
Corridor of memories..
Magic wand of time..
Is waved somewhere..
I begin to run backward...
Away from myself...
Towards you?
Twilight it is..
Somewhere in-between..
Day and night..
Time freezes...
I freeze...!

Every evening same story..
By night all settles down...
My breath renews its life...
I live on, again..
Onto a new tomorrow...
Again waiting...
For a memorable new evening!

Words!

Today my words are flowing..
I have no control over them..
They dance... they create..
They throb... they exist...
Am not incomplete today...
Am full to the brim..!
The beauty once you had given..
Is reflecting today...
In my words and me...
Come and see..
Come and feel..
How my words seal..
You in a symphony..
You in a rhythm...
You in a piece of music...
Each word of mine...
Tuned... and framed..
For you, in you..
Or else, words are sound..
Mere noise.. from which
Ashes rise..
Today they are poetry..
Beautiful and complete!

Complete!

I... a whole I, tucked in your arm,
When I bore nothing, but you,
In my eyes, in my heart,
In my breath, a you..
Entwined I was,
In you..
Like that creeper,
Of money plant..
Which cuddled the grills
Of my balcony..
I lay numb..
Dead to my own sensations..
Nothing kept me alive,
But your touches..
Like a baby..
Sleeping in mother's womb..
I slept in you...
Where, untimely separation...
Called for death...
Even separated... we are one...
One whole of me...
In a part of you!

In Choice!

I choose to be with you..
In my reality and.. in my dream..
In my one life and.. hundreds after it..
In my senses and.. when I am out of it..
In my laughter and..in my tears..
In my sorrow and.. as much in my joy..
In my giving and..in my receiving..
In my heart eternal and..in my body perishing..
In my leisure and...when am working..
In my words and.. in my silence...
In my creation and..when I construct nothing..
In my walks in the morning and.. in idle evening...
In my routine day and.. in my haphazard night..
In my beginnings and.. in all my ends..

I choose to be with you..

Concealed!

Oh my hidden love,
You are the pearl in my tears...
You a sparkle in my smile..
You a beat in heart's core..
You my air, when I breathe for a while..!
You are the shimmer in my champagne..
You the lustre in my glass of wine..
You are the colour in my drunken eyes..
You are my lonely night's shine..
You are the feeling of first spring day..
You the morning winter chill...
You my warmth in summer days..
You my rain on window-sill!
You are hues on my garden blooms..
You are the my joy in butterfly..
You are the infinite in finite me..
You are the ocean, where I have lost "I"!

Love!

That evening, life was full..
Full to the brim...
One touch deep within..
Woke me up..
From slumber of years..!
That stirred my soul..
And Am still awake..
Years after that..
My eyes bereft of slumber..
Devoid of dreams...
Stares at nothing..
Oh if this is love..
Let none tread onto it..
It cheats, it lies..
True it is not..
Take a leaf, from my book..
And breathe awhile...
Love not... love none...
It only kills..!

Freedom

Him that I love..
Today I set free..
From all I have..
From every part of me..
Today I open my arms..
Not to close again...
In love... I know now..
There's no end.. nowhere to begin..
The more I hold...
More it escapes...
Like ether in the palm...
Vanishes.. no forms it has... no shapes...
I wash myself from within...
Anew I am left in me..
Happiness of him.. only matters...
To my locked lips... its the only key!
Nothing remains far or near...
Except some memories about to fade...
Yet... if this world is a world of fire...
My few moments of bygone love is the shade...
I know not, what I pen...
I do not know my life...
Long I have been dead to myself...
Only to my love am alive...!

Longings!

At this moment:

My head needs the comfort of your shoulder..
My eyes longs for your face..
My skin craves for your touch..
My ears desires your voice..
My fingers wants to be locked in yours..
My lips trembles..
My heart beats in yours..
My smile vanishes in your lips..

This morning..
Coming noon..
Then the evening...
Then the night whole...

My longings never change..!

Rebirth!

That night, do you remember..
How the moon danced..
The stars swayed in the mid-sky!
Were they drunk like us?
That night, when the time halted..
In us... time froze..
I sought comfort... in your eyes..
You sought love.. in my heart..
That night was beautiful..
That night, I submerged in you..
And you emerged from my soul..
We both were born again!

Last Night!

Last night the winter sky..
Sparkled.. like a glass..
Filled with champagne..
Each star appeared drunk..
Moon was absent...
Not a trace of it there...
I watched on!
Night deepened like my heart..
From midnight to past it...
Time ticked away..
In my wrist...
I could not think..
Neither of me... nor of you..
All memories haphazard..
Suddenly one star fell...
I know not where...
I wished on it...
Then, like a child..
Playing hide and seek..
I came to get a peep..
Had gone to see you...!
Tip-toed I walked..
Scared the world may..
Be disturbed in its slumber...
I went to see you..!
Yes.. I did see..
A awakened me..
Within the lids..
Of your closed eye!

Sealed Soul!

What more could the year
Give or take?
Had given me hypnotized heart..
Where you the magician..
Shall live forever..
And a perished soul..
Which is void..
Closed... forever...
No more entries or exits!
Its sealed.. my soul!

You An Illusion, I A Dupe!

Heart a memory keeper..
Soul reverts back to past..
Goes back, stays there..
As if it shall forever last..!
Years come in, and pass by..
A day again becomes night..
Yet those golden glow..still,
Transmits from fading light!
Nothing to hold on..
Time, some sand on palm..
I write, re-write my story..
Within me a storm, outside calm!
Yet again, I start to live..
Yet again, that you breathe..
Some sky and cloud above us..
And a lot of earth, beneath!
Living together, far away..
Hoping against hope..
A slice of life escapes in gasp..
You an illusion, I a dupe!

Love Anew!

Above the defining words..
Petty and light..
I keep you in silence..!
Far from all falsity..
Away from denials all..
I accept you.. in my soul..!
I continue to fall in love..
And remain in love..
Everyday, once again..!
Beyond the gasping eyes..
Transcending the grasping mind..
I see you, waiting..!
That which began oneday..
Searched its end..
Found, a new beginning!
After a day fall..
With a new sunrise..
Love shines in a drop of dew!

Love forgets to fade and die..
Everyday it emerges anew!!

~Manjuri~

Traveller's Song

World that I have travelled..
I have toured far and near..
Under the sky full of clouds
Or on a day bright and clear..!

Sometimes by the dreamy brook..
Sometimes to the purple hill..
Oneday beating the summer heat..
Again braving the winter chill..!

Many springs I did spend..
Gazing at blooming bower..
Many monsoon I did drench..
Under a sky-breaking shower!

I travelled, and travelled..
To reach nowhere at all..
I shall continue to journey..
Till I end, or world comes to halt!

Empty Love!

Love, like a fragrant flower,
Lingers on..long after..
It has withered!
Love, like a spring storm..
Haunts.. long, long after..
Calm has set in!
Love, like an opera concert..
Rings on... long after..
The tunes has ended!
Love. like a glass of vodka..
Intoxicates... long after...
The glass empties...!
Love, like me... foolish me..
Continues to love.. long after..
You are gone...!

Stranger!

Stranger, do I know you, still?
That you had arrived once..
Out of the clear blue sky..
You eyes shone like the stars..
An alien you seemed..
Different from rest I knew..
As if from planet Mars..
You had dawned.. upon me..
Upon my onetime rich heart..

Stranger, do you know me, still?
That I had arrived once..
From the clouds of June sky..
That smile I brought.. on your lips..
That tune I gave, to your voice..
That lyrics I gave.. to your pen..
Now no more.. neither near, nor far..
Neither gone... nor remain.. some traces..
Of a stranger You loved, a stranger I loved!

A Call

Hold me.. for last and once..
Will you, hold me once?
Am too drunk to walk alone...
Life is slipping from me..
Am out of myself..
Will you hold me for this last time?
I know not, who I am..
Nor where Am I now..
Come to me... flow in me..
Be my sense for a while!
Mix in my blood..
Flow in my vein..
Be my pulse for a while...
Be my heart, be my soul..
You be me for a while..
Come be me.. to feel me..
Feel my pain within...
Be me to know me..
Come and be me for a while!
I may not open my eyes again..
Or I may not close to sleep...
And in both ways I lose you...
I may not see, nor dream you again!
So, be mine tonight... be as drunk as me..
Lose everything to find me...
As I did the same... to find you, in me!

Awake!

I lie awake, no, not very far..
Not very far from you..
I lie awake!
I lie awake, with my dream..
I lie awake with nourished soul..
I lie awake..
I go unsaid.. I go untold..
I lie awake with my generous heart..
Awake to give all the gifts..
I lie awake, amid a treasure boat..
Awake, sailing, with wants and needs!
I lie awake, beholding the beauty all..
Awake, burning in eternal fire..
Awake as I give away my spirit..
To your divine pyre!
I lie awake, among dust and smoke..
Awake, among ashes and soil..
Awake in words of syllable..
I was awake, long time back..
Today am awake as well..
In years to come, shall you find me..
Awake, for you, lost in your casted spell!

Still..

Do you read my poems,
To erase pain with pain?
Do you alloy in my lines,
To survive and to sustain?
I know, you still wait for me,
Its you, who still go numb,
As you hold a drink at night,
And read to say, 'it's a poetry'?
You fear, my lines may bleed,
As you, with smoky eyes read,
Some words, in the chest of time!
Still wait to read the last line,
Where I say, where I still say,
In spite of all, you are still mine..
Yes, somewhere within me...
Beyond my speculation..
Away from all calculation..

You still remain mine!

Treasure Trove

Buried within..
Is a treasure trove..
Filled to the brim..
It sparkles..
No, not diamond or pearl...
Nor gold has it, or silver..
Its light, is of love.
Once you had given,
Only once I had taken..
Giving ended..
Receiving goes on..
Each day I renew..
That which I got..
My love, refills itself..
My treasure trove..
Always full!
As I sit alone..
And evening arrives..
Lights me up..
Memories tip-toes in..
You slip into my soul..
Open my treasure trove..
Fill up my senses..
And then leave!
Tonight, if you decide to go..
Go, but with a promise..
Tomorrow you shall give..
Give me the key..
The key to my soul..
Key to my heart's treasure trove!

In Search Of Myself!

Am leaving in search of myself,
Alone I shall walk..
If I find myself, I shall be back..
Or, I shall never again, return!

I will continue, to walk by the shore,
In search of none but me,
I shall find myself someday..
By fully losing myself, maybe!

I shall solve my mystery own..
And remove my own soul's veil..
Now in search of me let me go..
If I return, I shall tell you my tale..!

I shall die within, many a times,
And, this death shall on me shine,
And I shall rise from my ashes own,
And if I find myself, I shall again be thine!

Being Myself!

Sweet is the intoxication..
That flows from my eyes..
And I get drowned..
In my tears own...
Sweet is the intoxication..
Which numbs my veins..
And I get frozen..
Within myself..
Sweet is the intoxication..
Which echoes in the air..
Like some late night music..
The sound of a mouth-organ..
Sweet is the intoxication..
That keeps me hidden..
From my own eyes..
Only to be sought by you..
Sweet is the intoxication..
Which gives me a lease of life..
Each night.. when I thought..
I was no more alive..
Sweet is the intoxication..
When I leave all..
To be with you..
And never come back..

Sweeter is the heaven, in which I dwell..
In peace, in love, and in utmost joy of being
myself!!

My Love, Do Come!

Oh love, fill my senses up..
Fill to the brim..
Nothing more I long for..
But your touch..
In my dream..
Come slowly.. tip-toeing
Come to my heart..
I have never left you..
Love, its you...
You... who moved apart..
Come tonight..
Am alone in my garden..
Bring me no flower..
Sensing your arrival
Blooms graced my bower...
Come love...
Come alone...
Bring none with you
Am alone only with myself
So be you!
Am drunk as the moon above..
Am shining bright too
Some say its my inner glow..
Only I know its my love
Shining for you!

~Manjuri~

Heart This Autumn Morning!

Autumn morning,
Like a childhood friend,
Hugs my soul...
Tide of memories
Washes me from myself..
What I left behind,
My days of galore..
My mornings of bounty,
Evenings complete...
A me, from far hills,
Now watches the wave..
Smiling at my fate..
Like that ebb, that comes in,
Then, goes away..
I sway..

With all that is transient
In me and my being..
All that I once held so dear
Now far they appear..
My eyes gathers smoke..
As I wake..
To a lonely autumn morning,
Far from my heart..
Far from home..
Making me realize..
Those and that we love..
Does not go away..
They remain within..
For us to play..
As solitude gathers..
Like winter mist..
Heart takes a plunge..
And comes out refreshed..
Beautifully alive again!

Winter Nights

Night's clock ticks,
Time run towards you,
I flow..
I reach..
Open the door..
Am knocking!
Its cold outside..
Its snowing..
Allow me to sit..
By the fire-place..
Ignite the lamp!
This moment is beautiful!
From night to midnight..
Hours become minutes..
Minutes becomes seconds..
Time stops..
World halts..
My step in your house..
Froze forever..
After the snow..
When sun shall shine..
Nothing shall melt..
I place word after word..
I darn all that is torn..
With my poetry..
I stitch my soul..
With your love..
Its snowing outside..
Take me in, open the door..
Am waiting..!

No Blooms, No Wither!

I cannot love you any more..
Cannot love you less either..
My heart full to the brim..
Nothing now blooms or wither!

I cannot stop loving you,
Cannot begin again..
Each beat within talks of you,
My heart says you remain!

I cannot walk to you,
Cannot walk away too..
You come once to see me..
And know how I live without you!

I cannot tell you in words,
Cannot bear in silence as well..
Far in your sky, a star I am..
That once shone and fell!

I cannot breathe in..
Cannot breathe out my blue..
For, all I had, and all I have..
Begin and ends in you!

~Manjuri~

Reflection!

When my reflection rippled in you,
I blushed seeing my own face..
It was not me...
It was you..
Caressing me with your breathe..
Where is the difference?
What is you, I am that..
You a picture, am a reflection..
You a voice, am the echo..
You the sky, am a star..
Never separate, hardly far..
I asked for your heart..
So that I keep it in my rib-cage..
It beat as me..
Ahh... no difference..
Neither of kind... nor of degree..
I am you... you are me!

Dissolved Reverie!

Last night I was with you..
Moon was veiled..
Light was dim..
I stood beyond the stars..
Leaning onto you..
Night drank from our eyes..
We hummed a song..
A melody was born..!

No words spoken,
No voice heard..
Myriad hues of sky-flowers..
Bloomed in our soul..
For a while..
Afar from all..
Two hearts thrived..
As one..!
A little before dawn..
My dream was gone..
Space vanished in space..
I faded into you..
Nothing remained anywhere..
Washed and cleansed my spirits..
Awaits for another night..
For a reverie to get life..!
Again shall it come..
To live for a night..
Before it dissolves..
Into the heart of eternity!

Intoxicated!

Slowly very slowly
I slip into nothing,
Senses numb,
Vision blurs..
World a paradise!
Smile infects my lips..
I hug my memories..
The September moon..
Shines on my skin..
For a moment..
You emerge..
Wearing a silver glow..!
You sink..
Into my soul..
I shut my soul up..
Closing all the routes..
Of your escape..
Trapped you sleep..

Like a baby..
Within me..!
They say I am drunk..
Intoxicated is my spirits..
Let what they say, be true..
Oh my drunken self..
How beautiful is this me..
In my senses what I abort..
Comes back to love me..
When I am out of it..!
Oh how divine is this..
This senseless..
This useless..
This loving me!!

Last Answer!

What doubt shrouds your soul?
Where have you lost your faith?
Can you not distinguish anymore?
Between reality and alluring myth?

Why you say our roads are parallel?
Why do you call it separate?
Why can you not feel like me?
That our heart beats at an equal rate!

You have too many questions,
Answer I have no new..
All I got to say, with all senses on,
Its you I know, I love you!

I Have Not.. I Shall Not..!!

I have not loved anyone, this very much..
As I loved you..
Nor shall I ever love anyone, so very much..
As I loved you..
I have not longed for anyone, this very much..
As I longed for you..
Nor shall my heart ache, so very much...
As it ached for you..
I have not smiled, this very much..
As I smiled with you..
Nor did I weep for anyone, so very much..
As I have wept for you..
I have not draped my words, this very much..
As I draped them for you..
Nor have I dressed in silence, so very much..
As I have dressed for you..

I have not.. I shall not..
I will not breathe for anyone else..
If you stop to be the air around me..
Let life pause on my arrested pulse..!

Grass And Leaf!

Like the grass that treasures,
The dead leaves..
I keep you in my bosom...
I pray each day..
No strong breeze should...
Sway you away...
Away from me...!
Like the fallen leaves..
Of mid-autumn..
You left home..
But could not leave the heart..
Could not move apart..
From near the tree..
To which you once belonged...!
I am but a stretch of grass...
You a leaf astray...
No wind shall be brave enough..
To take you away...
Away from me!

In Love Again!

Am feeling tender again..
Today am feeling you..
The blowing breeze..
Touched me, making me new...

Like that flower dainty..
Am too fragile in love...
Give me all you can tonight..
Pour on me all that you have...

Fading rays of dwindling sun..
Dupes me each evening fine..
Tell me once tonight..whisper that..
You too have fallen in love again!

Discovery!

I have caged myself,
In my own soul..
I have built a prison..
Locked up my emotion..
I have stoned my heart..
Nothing reaches me..
When you are apart..
I have numbed my senses..
And frozen my smile..
Even if I come back..
But for a while..
The call of unknown..
Will take me back..
I have nothing left..
Nothing to give or take..
Am empty as the sky..
As beneath it I lie..
Alone with the stars..
With thought that,
Begets smile..
But for a while..

I did come..
Only to go..
With no promise..
To be back..
Only some memories..
Carried on my backpack!
Journey begins..
Endless one..
If I reach, you shall know..
Or else, when remembrance..
Haunts you strong..
Do come along..
To find me you too got to leave..
What I left, in the loop of time..
To find me, get lost for once..
To get lost, do find me once!

Your Woman!

Your touch had once,
Made a woman out of me..

I realized, I was beautiful..
By the looks in your eyes...
I realized I was loved..
By the hidden smile..
That your lips flaunted..

My senses alert..
My heart throbbed in you..
My tears made your eyes..
Appear like a high tide ocean..

Oh! What a pleasure it had been..
To be your woman!

Becoming Love!

Who on earth told you,
To be a miser,
And hoard your love,
Only within you?
Is your heart a locker?
Where you put love,
Under safe custody,
Of lock and key!

Look within,
Your's is an ocean out there,
Waves are high, shore not far..
I got all wet!

Love is not a fragile emotion,
It lives in your breath,
In it goes, out it comes,
Each time you inhale and exhale..
You run from it, but you are clutched,
You are held by it, so much so that,
You have become it,
Yes, like me, you too have become love!

Eloquent Silence

Will meet you there,
Where no echoes exist,
Where, soul lies awake,
On a carpeted grass field...

Will meet you there...
Where we got nothing to learn..
Among thousand imperfections..
We shall still hold hands...

Will meet you there..
Where sky meets the earth...
Sailing in the tip of waves...
Beyond all futures and pasts...

Will meet you someday,
For a moment, beyond time,
Tranquil hearts, rhythmic beats,
We both, and complete peace!

Half-Truths!

Night deepens.. world fast asleep..
I lay awake.. thoughts grip..
My eyes, bereft of slumber..
Sees you.. as I spread them far..
I cannot move.. I become captive..
As if.. you are holding me.. tight..
From my body to my soul..
Your touch spreads.. I breathe..
You lend me your hand..
To drag me out..
Out of this locked abandoned house..
At the touch of your hand..
My skin quivers.. I live again..
To die a quite death, in a while..!
Night light gives birth to some long shadows..
I know not whose reflections they are..
Not of me, nor are they of you..
Those shadows are strange!
Robe of the soul has worn off..
Bare.. naked.. I am what I am.. to myself..
At the dead of night..
Yes, You came to see me, so did I..
Learn to fade with light..
Go away.. now go away...
Go away.. before smoke burns my eyes..
I shall wait again, this midnight..
I shall begin waiting with the fading light..
A wait.. again.. a wait for you to hold me tight!

My Last Verse!

My last verse, is engraved here,
My last verse for you..
My words have come to an end..
And nothing awaits a renew..
My emotions are hardened now..
Tear refuse to flow..
Yet I try and write, for you..
A verse, before I go..
Memories fade like twilight,
No feelings grip the heart..
Even the chirping birds sing,
Tunes of final depart..!
Cold lies the chimney ashes,
Fire long gone..
Time to move away from myself,
And hit the road alone..!
Withered lies my blooming bough,
Weeds rule the garden..
Who has left from here?
That heaven appears forsaken!
Silence screams at the dead of night,
As I let all exist and be..
And I pen this last verse..
For your eyes and that of me!

Love And Life!

Love held life's hand,
Pulled it to its chest..
Embraced it tight, said,
'In me you rest'!

Life said, 'let me go,
I am none to you..
I left living long back..
Now I shall die for you'!

Love smiled, said,
'Go if you can,
In my shadow you shall die,
As in me once you began'!

Sleepless Verse!

Last night it was well past four,
When all surrendered to sleep;
Wrapped themselves in peace,
Behind their four walls, shut doors.

I took a virtual flight, to see you,
Across the blue hills, azure sea;
I travelled, I carried myself, for me;
And did get a glimpse of divine you.

The stars were drunk and drowsy,
The moon wore cloud's warm blanket;
Sea slept wearing the wavy locket,
Roads were lonely, dark and grumpy.

I saw you in faded caliginous light,
Some shadow fell on your face;
Am hurrying, crossing a maze,
A madness at the dead end of night.

Beautiful night, rests in your slumber,
Innocent night, in my insomniac eyes;
Sees virtues all... denounces all vice,
Tries to pretend, to get lost in you forever.

Morning tiptoed in, treading upon my dreams,
Better senses dawned, with the rising sun;
I smiled on my folly own, now noon too is done,
In twelve hours, I passed a day it seems...!

Come Lets Flee!

I noticed a new footprint,
On the sand of time,
Who is it, that left a mark?
I thought, from behind!

A new boat was anchored,
On the shore of life,
But where is the boatman?
Who left love in rife!

A piece of new dark sky,
Was glooming above,
What is that song I hear?
Composed with love!!

A spread of ocean new, beyond,
This tarnished earth,
Who has spread wings to fly?
And carry me in all dearth!

A new shore, a new sea, a new,
Is all that I see,
You are renewed, so am I, and,
In new spirits lets flee!

Some Time!

Some wrinkles have I traced on the face of time,
Some very old desires I felt in it forever sublime!
Some that you had given me, but I could not keep,
Some that I had given you, but you lost them in
heap!

Some moments that are frozen in my mind's shot,
Some moments that you still contemplate may
be yet!

Some reminiscences of your memories still new
in me,
Some probably that you want to dis-remember of me!

Some eons of time, some era of our excellent
being,
Some that we had lived together, before our
leaving!

Some that we had let go on our wishes so
very own,
Some that we have retained in our hearts,
unknown!

Some parts that make us whole, some whole to
part,
Some beginnings yet to begin, some end yet to
start!

Some day down the street, in the veil of the light,
Some one dashes onto you, and you know all is
right;

Some knowledge shall dawn on you, and you know
that,
Some one who loved you once perhaps is not
dead yet!

Complete Existence!

On a midnight,
Far away, on the end of world,
There was a You and a I,
Hidden from all worldly eye..
We stole a few moments..
Stole some pearls,
From the string of time..
Some moments..
Where You and I..
Made that space and time..
Complete, by our existence..

Last midnight..
Far away, in another end of world..
I was alone,
Unaware I was..
Of my own existence..
Slowly I sipped in the goblet,
Filled with sparking memories..
Intoxication spread...
From heart to eyes...
I again, completed, my existence..

Hearty Autumn!

Dying once everyday,
I could not take,
Today I died,
Yes, for once and all!
May my end,
Mark a new start,
In your life,
..

Let me be blamed,
For this eternal autumn,
Leaves fall to grow..
But, this year..
No leaves shall grace,
The branches..
No spring shall come..

I leave, with fall,
In my heart..!

Wind Of Change!

Deep within me,
Something has awaken,
Sleeping, dormant, they were,
Lying idle for ages..
Eon passed, in my sleep.
Within the creases,
Of folded heart, I just saw,
A picture, imperfect,
Withered, languished..
I shivered in dismay
A chill ran down my spine,
This is me?
I thought for a while,
Paused, I wiped, my eyes,
For moisture laden they were,
My slumber is done,
Sleep all gone,
I am, alert, awake,
And in senses now.
Like the rays,
Of the shining dawn,
My inner, is now adorn.
A curtain raised, I get to see,
A glimpse of light, within me.
Dark clouds of the july sky,
Slowly that came by,
And spread itself,
Had fully eclipsed me.

Then came a gush of
Southerly wind,
Blew the clouds away,
Leaving me shining,
Like the evening's first star..
Oh the gust of wind unknown,
Listen to what I say,
I will not be the same again,
Never, the same,
As you have forever,
Changed my way!

My All In You!

You,
Are my drop-box,
Where I drop in my secrets,
Written in black ink,
None else can read them,
I dump into you,
And lock the box,
I lock in you,
An unknown part of myself!

You,
Are my treasure-house,
Million thoughts of,
Embellished fineness,
Priceless emotions,
My precious smiles,
Pearl-like tears,
I lock in you,
An exquisite part of myself!

You,
Are my attic on the roof,
From where each evening,
I watch the sun,
Drowning itself into the sea,
I sit inside you,
With book and music,
I lock in you,
An absolute part of myself!

You,
Are my open sky,
To whom, I speak,
My words of good,
And not so good,
In you I paint,
My hued clouds,
I lock in you,
An artist that I find myself!

Ethereal Existence!

Could that rainbow, be my bridge?
Crossing which, I reach you..
With seven colours I paint myself..
Rolling on its divine hue..!

Could those dry leaves, create my music,
Music of my heart's wait..
Patiently mingling into my untapped tune..
Unveiling you, Oh my soulmate...!

Could those clouds, be my carrier?
As I trespass the trap of time...
And they break into sky's tears..
When I see you amid rainy chime...!

Could that wave be my dance floor?
That one, with tallest tip..
As I dance for you, one mid-noon..
Sea, absorbing my silent weep..!

But,

Beyond all these could's and if's..
A me exists, not ethereal..
Unknown I, may shrink like a weed..
Known I, shine in your eyes pearl..!

Reincarnation!

As I open up to life,
Bit my bit,
Flowing eternally,
In the cascade of tunes,
Dancing, tapping,
To the rhythm of rain..
Oblivious for a while,
Of my own existence..
Transcending the realm,
Of a forbidden legacy..
A legacy, my heart,
Quietly bestows upon me..
None aware, none knows,
How I trespass myself,
To reach you, beyond yourself..
As I shine in your radiant love,
And as I share your gift,
With myself, none but myself,
Enriching all that is mine,
Including my essential being,
Which is ready for an incarnation..
Let me be born again.. in you!

All In Vague

A kind of vague longing,
That escapes with each sigh of soul,
A suppressed wail, that demands outbreak,
And you well up, in my memoirs, in my thoughts,
And my dream all..

An ardor tucked in heart's core,
Seeks some freedom but for a while,
I walk a mile alone, in the paved path of life,
As if my hands are held by you, and my lips,
Adorn your smile..

Song of love, tuned in youth, unheard by any
though,
Now dances in the blades of grass, in
morning dew..
Reverberating, echoing, across the memory lane..
Fluttering away in joy, on that deserted path,
Visited by very few..

Scintillating stars, waves of sea, million grains of
sand,
A moon, a sun, and all that are sworn in to promise
love..
All shall perish, all shall end, all shall sleep in the
tomb of time..
But my wait, my vague emotions, and me shall
forever soar,
Like that white dove...

Strange Ordeal!

Sometimes,
Its my shadow,
Which carries me..
I exist,
Only in my dark reflection.
When time sleeps,
In the lap of earth,
And I, awake..
Behind the locked gate,
Of my own consciousness..
I trip, fall, and rise..
While,
A night that passes,
In strange ordeal!

~Manjuri~

River of Dreams!

A new river, and its new bank..
Time yet to writ its tale..
Beyond all happiness of human soul,
And above all its wail...

A flow of new aqua,
Tearing the heart of earth..
A hand-full of new mud..
That lay on the red path..

Few blooms, that were fresh,
Along the bay of life..
Destined to wither in a day or two..
While some newer get to thrive..!

In my dreams did I see,
A new cause of living..
It was beautiful, hued hopes,
Yonder from breathing or existing..

None knew, none aware,
My river of dreams flew by..
On its bank, I lived, with myself,
And a pair of waiting eyes!

A Lover's Note

I left myself behind,
As I began to walk,
With you..
I forgot my own being,
As I began to live,
In you..
I submitted to silence,
As I gave my words,
To you..
I got drunk, by inhaling air,
As the air was scented,
By you..
I laughed, in joy utmost,
As my laughter roared in cloud,
For you..
I wailed in pain unknown
As my tears are dropped,
By you..
I am the richest on this earth,
As, I know, I am aware, I,
Have you..
I am dead, no trace of me remains,
As I merge, my body and soul,
Into you.

Again..

Moon, a full one,
Appeared like a glass goblet,
Filled with sparkling white wine..
I sipped little by little..
Got drunk..
Moon my goblet, moon my wine..
This evening in my solitude..
Me and my moonlit sky..
Intoxicated, I lie numb,
Impaired I am now,
To my own feelings..

Only my throat choked,
With the unsaid words,
Words, that I had kept,
Only for you..!
Then I slept,
In a deep slumber..
I passed in time,
Time passed in me..
I dreamt..
I lived in my dream..
I breathed till my reverie lasted..
Now am awake..
Carrying some imprints..
Some crumbs fallen..
From that crispy dream..
Deep within me..

Today too an evening shall come..
Again the moon shall rise..
I shall drink the moon again..
Dream again... live again..
Be in solitude again..
Frozen me shall melt again..!
In solitude!

Wild Flower!

A flower that bloomed,
A wild flower,
Hidden from the gardener's eye..
Flourished, unloved, uncared for,
Among the weeds, for a while...
Today it withered, perished,
No traces remain..
Gardener ignorant, unknown,
Flower that he did not see..
In his garden own..!
A dead wild beauty..
Only the mosses,
And a few weeds,
Who saw her for a day...
Are sad, in pain..
Tugged in the corner,
In utter dismay!

Note To Myself!

Submitted to emptiness,
Given to the void within,
Nothing to hold on,
Nothing to clutch for living...
Soiled is the heart's core,
With memories yet to erase,
Why to hold on? What to hold on?
Questions that soul do raise..
Stampede of many emotions,
Rampage that grips the soul,
When I want to pelt a stone,
And break that shining moon...
When I want to lay my head,
Onto this earth's muddy lap..
When I want to sleep,
In that mossy doorstep...
Love had come once,
But I could not hold,
It left without taking,
Leaving me richer, manifold..
Now in my unloved hour,
When am alone and void,
I know, all are but illusions fine,
Only, I to myself have cheated!

Loving Within!

When heart lives on the edge,
Soul almost vanquished,
Pulse sinks in its own ticks,
And living languished..

When eyes drowns on its aqua own,
Cheeks pale and blue,
And lips get your name frozen,
Moments searching you in tiniest clue..

When giving awaits with all its gifts,
But taking closes its receiving door,
And when richness gets richer,
By losing all in love no more..

When pain leaves the body numb,
Blood denies to flow in the vein,
When win and lose are but synonyms,
And no difference lies between loss and gain...

At that moment of some strange living,
When I am anything but me,
In silence, I do realize, each time,
I am loving you, inside me!

Memoirs..

Some fragments of myself,
Scattered within you,
Some pieces of broken you,
Still lies within me..
Do come and see..
I have not gathered them,
Nor did I try and mend..
Beautifully we do exist,
In each other's fragment!
You had your share of pain,
I had mine too..
But in my each thought..
I got diffused in you!
Our paths have never crossed,
Nor it awaits an affair..
Yet in its relentless wait,
Days became months, and,
Months long became years..
That road we once took,
To reach each other..
Lies broken, almost like us..
And the eden
In which we once sat,
Holding hands..
Both in love and in regret..
Now sleeps in weeds..
Yet sometimes: when..
Flowers do bloom, and wither..
None thinks of us, none remember...

We are erased from there, forever..
I have noticed, as I pass,
Crack appeared on the bench..
Yet the air there is still loaded..
And also are memoirs, trapped in trench!

Amidst Nothing!

Beyond myself, a piece of me,
Why still it longs for thee?
Amidst something, nothing remained,
You and I in bond unnamed!

Deep within, somewhere unknown,
A little want, small passion,
Surfaces at the dead of night,
Thoughts ignite!

A touch, a single one, long ago,
I carry as your logo,
Your warmth transferred, in hands of mine,
Still beautiful, still divine!

You gave me nothing, nothing to love,
Still I treasured, nothing that I have,
No renewal was ever done,
Yet this love, remains, never is gone!

Today I wish, with almost my all,
Somber me sans enthrall,
If ever storm seeks refuge in your heart too,
Come over, for Am still waiting for you!

Beyond Complaints One Day!

Someday you write something for me,
You never spend your words on me,
Yes I complaint!

Someday you sing for me, only me,
You never spare your tunes for my ears,
Yes I complaint!

Someday you too stay awake, for me,
But your nights never included me,
Yes I complaint!

Someday, come and meet me, for once,
But your roads never lead you to me,
Yes I complaint!

Someday, drop a few tears for me too,
But your eyes are never moist for me,
Yes I complaint!

Someday, pick those white blooms,
And place them on my tombed home,
I shall never complaint!

Thus with me, ends my complaints all!
My heart says you live on,
Beyond my complaints and me!

A Summer Again!

The sun is scorching,
Sand burns in heat,
It is the waves,
That rise and fall,
With my each heart-beat!

Far far in that horizon,
Where my eyes stretch to reach,
I find you no more,
Hidden behind the clouds,
Or fathomed in shore beneath!

Summer comes, summer goes,
Spring is not eternal either,
It is me whose relentless wait,
Makes all the seasons equal,
And in all, you and I forever loiter!

A Wish!

I want to be a piece of cloud,
A vagabond by birth,
Floating on my pace own,
Far away from this earth!

None to resist my reckless flight,
None to call me home,
Oh! What a mirth it would be,
Flying all alone!

I could flirt with the wind strong,
Gaze at that loving moon,
Stars and sun would be close by,
Yet, my freedom of being alone!

Then I would get heavy one day,
And would want to pour down,
My joys would be droplets then,
Dropping all alone!

From brooks to rivers I would flow,
And from rivers to that sea,
Again in vapours I would rise,
And again float in cloudy glee!

If I do become a cloud someday,
And get my lone flight,
I would come to see you oneday,
However you try and hide!

I shall catch you unaware,
As you gaze at me,
Wondering, 'oh this cloud, I know,
Does it not look like she'!

I shall smile at your folly,
You knew not, it was me,
And the joy of seeing you...
A cloud, someday, I must be!

Shadow Of The Heart!

When darkness deepens, at dead of night,
And the globe gets lost, in its shadow own,
My ears gets haunted, and my senses filled,
When I devour, annihilate, and get lost in,
A faint, long lost voice from domain unknown!

Aberration dissolves, between pain and joy,
Tears that flow from eyes, gets its due worth,
Love, remains coffined in my caged soul,
For, I know, this shall not end, I know,
After a death, I shall get an awaited re-birth!

Again a fresh course of pain shall resume,
A trust to be throttled and killed again,
And abandoned love shall seek path,
A story shall renew itself, get started,
To end again, in the shadow of its own heart!

Two Nights, True Colour!

On your lonely night of pain utmost,
When your shadow left you,
And you called me aloud,
I ran bare foot, left myself behind,
To be with you..
For a while...
Holding hands in turmoil...!

On my lonely night, when my pulse stopped,
I opened my painful eyelids,
In search of you..
Knocked slowly on your closed pane,
Door did not open....
I am awakened, and, besides me,
My dream, pieced and broken!

Valentine's Note!

Softly when all feelings settle within, and,
Some reminiscence of my own pain reflects,
I turn my eyes towards the sky, and,
All oblivion, all forgotten, again recollects!

Unspoken words lingers within silence,
Unexpressed feelings grips me,
Your pain, echoed within me today,
And I knew, you were never meant for me!

A numbness, an inertia grips my soul,
Thousand feelings just got frozen!
Oh how beautiful are love's facets,
In love, within love, all happily happen!

The droplets fell on my palm own,
As the swollen capsules gives up,
And, from my flowing eyes I know,
Love allows no holding back,..
For In Love :
Its only giving all and giving up!

Fragile Dream!

It was not so long ago,
That in you I felt myself echo,
Now what remains,
Are sounds, of an alien domain!

My pain, my joy, my me,
Never knew how and when they left me,
They all had built a nest,
In your soul, far away, from my own zest!

I owned nothing, all given,
Believed, trusted, you had all taken,
Faith of love kept me green,
But then, how much life has a dream?

Your pain weighs more,
It slices you and your heart's core,
My pain is but gesture light,
Weightless, as the bird's wings on its flight!

Only Question Remains!

The dried red rose, that,
Still serves as a bookmark,
Once you had bought for me,
Without any occasion special,
Only on a heart's call...
Was it love?

That sketch you made for me,
On the reverse of an empty,
Cigarette packet, some motifs,
Of your puzzled mind, and said,
Keep it, for someday, I may not be,
Was it love?

Those walk down the haphazard lanes,
On chilled winter evenings, foggy,
Misty, gloomy, yet, warm with feelings,
Reasons unknown, destination unreached,
Saw a brighter moon, stars had glitter more,
Was it love?

Countless waits, numberless annoy,
Speechless days passed in agony,
Known facts, unbelievable truths,
Hidden, camouflaged from all eyes,
A fragile trust of belonging, till the end,
Was it love?

Years passed by, time did not wait,
It was only me waiting relentlessly,
Still I wait... thousand years gone...
Answer duped me... like ever...
No answer, for, silence never speak,
Was it love?

Only question remains!!!

On An Autumn Rendezvous!

The sky has washed its gown,
Its blue has been bleached,
Clouds have gone vagabond,
Announcing, autumn has reached!

My heart dances in delight alien,
My senses have stepped out of me,
A kind of bewilderment haunts,
And, the 'I' just got to run and flee!

Festive mood flows in the air,
A call from bosom deep beckon,
Am off on a rendezvous folks,
Am off as I hear some song forlorn!

My backpack carries nothing at all,
My soul bereft of all that once burdened,
Yes, this journey I shall make for myself,
Solely with myself, and some memoirs hardened!

Back To Back!

One star studded night,
By the dreamy beach,
We sit, back to back,
You lean on me, I on you,
The waves are loud,
And the moon is new!
Time took a pause,
My eyes are filled,
So is yours, as we sit,
Back to back, on the beach!
Silence gets to say,
In its enchanting way,
Ripples generate,
In my blood, echoes in veins,
I fall back on you, again!
Sleep slips in my eyes,
Yet I am awake, for,
Thousand years now!
Tell me how, you sleep,
As I lay awake even in slumber!
That night on the beach,
As we sit, back to back,
With entangled breath,
In the cold sea breeze,
We sit, we wonder,
We dream, we say to each other,
I a wave, you a wave,
We mix, we are the sea,
You and me, that night,
Sit back to back, on the beach!

Nothing!

Nothing is all I have...
Nowhere to go!
No mind exists in me...
No form.... no existence,
Nothing I can relate to...
Nothing to show...!
No words I have...
Nothing to speak or tell..
No love, no joy.. suddenly...
Nothing becomes a 'me'...
Nothing places me right, but a,
Nothing from you...
Nothing.. absolutely...
Nothing from you!

Timer!

Time, a great player,
It breaks my life,
Into puzzle pieces!
Then whispers,
Assort them now,
Keep them, well,
In their places!!

I, stand still,
Gazing at the horizon,
Believing, all that I want,
To see, is written there!
But, the sky a virgin paper,
Where I paste my pictures,
An imaginary collage,
A fake assortment,
Of living and giving!

Time, returns in a while,
Smiles, asks, 'solved'?
I say, no not yet,
Am still repaying the,
Debts of life, with life,
Once am done, shall,
Pick up the pieces,
And place them right!!

Time, smiles, says,
'I will wait till eternity,
But, the day, all shall,
Get solved and placed,
You shall be beyond,
All the realizations great!!'

Love Story!

The moon slept, with the million stars,
Earth slept, so did venus and the mars,
All the planets took a slumber deep,
The clouds came in to sneak a peep,
Saw the sky was still awake, and told,
Sleep now dear sky, we shall unfold,
Spread like a warm quilt upon you all,
Relax, and slowly asleep, you got to fall!
Sky sighed, and smiled to tell the clouds,
How can I sleep you all got to tell me aloud,
My sun is awake in some corner of my heart,
I cannot close my eyes, sleep is well still far!
Clouds stood a witness to this story whole,
Today it told me, hence I retell it to you all!
Love lies is its power of thousand fold giving,
Ask the sky, and know, what it is to be loving!

Moments Of Solitude

In a moment of complete solitude,
When humble, without attitude,
When the heart is devoid of all ego,
It then lives in past, days long ago;
Tries to break all given rules of life,
Of all its haves, and all deprives,
Counting on its joyful blessings all,
Whispering, alluring, in my ears own,
Telling me slowly, that, life is beautiful!!
Trying to convince my inherent self,
Am better off, than, anyone else;
Many have less, than treasure mine,
Many have much more, but that's fine;
The stars, the moon and the sun one,
Are solely mine, I share with none;
The bird that sings, but only for me,
And what my eyes behold, are for me;
Rest, whatever exiguous do I possess,
In the crease of heart, when compress,
Of my God, of my divine, pure line soul,
That supreme being, now my only goal,
I give you all I have, you must accept,
My exit, lies in all your denial and reject!

A Story Of Thousand!

Thousand miles I have walked..
For over a thousand years..
Thousand valleys did I cross..
Over thousand hills, I did march..!

Thousand of rivers did I swim across..
Wrapped in thousand sands of desert..
Thousand storm did I brave..
Amongst a thousand alerts...!

Thousand winters did I pass..
A thousand spring I did hear sing..
Autumn fall did I witness a thousand..
And a summer thousand I kept within..!

Thousand questions I answered..
Thousand eyes looked and gone..
Thousand times did I tell them..
Amidst all thousands, you are the One!

Thousand lights might have shone..
Lighting a thousand path..
For me its you, one flickering lamp..
Illuminating my world, my earth..!

Thousand births did I live and die,
Another thousand yet to come..
But I shall wait in thousand ways..
Before am gone, all at once!

A Gift!

Where spirit hugs the faith,
Smiling even in tear..
All it knows is, it is loved..
And have nothing to fear!

Beyond all mundane words
Where my love grows in silence,
I kept one flower hidden for you..
Whose appeal is timeless!

Come slowly, tip-toeing..
Come invisible to eyes all..
For wrapped in it, am gifting..
Am gifting you.. my soul!

Love It Is!

Coloured by my blood,
It beats, beats as my heart..
It sways in the twilight..
My love.. my crimson love..
Nourished it is... by my soul..
It flourished away from me..
So love it must be!!
It too has an inferno within..
It too probably burns..
Like the sun...
Blazed to light all..!!
Unseen it goes to many a eye..
Unknown to many spirits..
But it bloomed..
Love it must be..!
Night approaches..
Blows in death..
It disappears,
So does its shadow!
No traces left..
Only I know..
It had once come..
So, love it must be!
Love it is!

A Drop Of Ocean!

Am a transient drop of water..
You the vast chest of earth..
Let me fall on you and vanish..
As you wait in utter dearth..!

You may not know, when I formed..
Nor when I dropped to die..
Unnoticed, unknown I come and go..
Everyday.. every moment.. I pass by!

Again and again, I form to break..
Again I shall end, all shall see..
As all know am but a drop of rain..
Only to you a Ocean, I want to be!

Mark Time!

Frozen time about to melt,
Upon the lap of earth,
You have changed, so did I,
Only same remains, our waiting path!

Season come in and move away,
Blazed flowers bloom to shed,
I wait, from where I was..
While you deny to tread!

The boat that was anchored for us,
Now rusts in its own pain,
And with each lash of fresh wave..
Yet another wait begins!!

Departing Note!

I know not what I take along,
Nor am I aware of what I leave behind,
Heart is insensate, somewhat numb,
Eyes are shut, almost blind!

Neither am I sad, I can say,
Nor am I weeping in silence,
That which lies frozen within,
Are your laughter and your glance!

Oh hills! what spell thou have cast,
I long no more for shore or tide,
Within my soul's core, you smile,
Its you who are there, rest all aside!

The purple branches of Jacaranda,
Or the pink ones of Cherry Blossom,
All appear so very proxime to me,
As if they bloomed within my bosom!

The enduring call of the alluring pine,
Or that eternal murmur of the brook,
How can I resist tell me? And I,
Find myself glued, securely hooked!

A century old, my ancient home,
Still erect, with stories in its heart,
Pictures within my mind's eye,
As I set myself, set to depart!

Mourn not my going away,
Cry not Oh clouds, drip not as rain,
I am accustomed to this sojourn,
And its associated pain!

Setting sun shall call it a day,
Rising one shall begin anew,
Everything will remain, in the hills,
Only I shall leave, bid adieu!

Without me the hills shall survive,
But how shall I without them?
Call me not, Oh! the the southern sea,
At last tears roll, and I am overwhelmed!

Setting Sun!

I hardly keep my eyes open these days,
For you, I keep them close,
You are far away in my awaken state,
I find you deep within, in my muse!

Setting sun, promises new day,
It vows a everyday return,
Hardly does it know, without you,
Even my days are sans sun!

Song of waves are not heard anymore,
Not because shore has gone deaf,
But I am gone out of tune,
Echoing in my own life's gap!

Winter is ready to depart,
Spring's cuckoo began to sing..
Fallen leaves are luckier than me,
For they await a replenish!

Behind this dusk a night waits,
Waits to be ripen by starry touch,
Yet all falls to meet my wait,
My wait for you is so very much!

Heart speaks, heart listens,
It is heart who writes,
This verses of setting sun,
Only for your closed eyes!

Inverted Walks!

One day the clouds thought,
How boring is this blue sky,
So they came down to earth,
Curbing their wish to fly!

They strolled on the branches,
Above the lake of glass,
Oh how beautiful the world is,
They thought thus!

I sat for a while, and thought,
If clouds can, why not I?
To reach you, someday,
I shall walk across the sky!

Mind Language!

Oh mind, why do you swing,
Like that girl hanging in the,
Trapeze..
Come with me, sit for a while,
Empty yourself, of all thoughts,
Freeze..
Oh my mind, come lets go,
Together, on a rendezvous,
Bliss..
Let us go, where no men went,
In that land nothing remains, all,
Cease..
On that voyage over the sea,
Or adventure, treading alp,
Peace..
You, I, and our heart and soul,
Rest all that we shall carry are on,
Lease..
Oh, the thought of it, gives me joy,
Mind, mind you, now its time for our,
Flees..

Being Choice-less!

Among a million feelings
That grips my lone heart,
I picked up one that I trust,
We are close, not apart!

Among the countless faces,
I pick the one, I want to see,
Your glance, your smile, and,
Its always, forever, you for me!

Crossroads Of Life!

Which road do I tread?
To reach onto you?
I have no map of life..
And these roads appear new!

Its morning now, fresh and green,
And the sun as usual is up,
Noon shall come, then evening,
Followed by a night which is dark!

I lit a lamp, to light my path,
But the wind is ruthless and strong,
I know, before I reach you,
My lamp's light shall be gone!

Then in dark, almost blind,
I shall walk following my heart,
Wait there, Oh my love,
No puzzled road can keep us apart!

I Love You!

I love you in my silence,
Love you in my words too,
I love you with all I have,
And with all that makes me you!

I love you with my everything,
And with my nothing as well,
I love you, in all possible ways,
That's all I want to tell!

I love you with myself,
And when am out of me,
I love you with my unseen vision,
And with all that I can see!

I love you, as much as you know,
And much beyond you realize,
Am loving you today, tomorrow,
And shall, till death beckons, and I die!

Deluged Self!

Abyssal within, a touch sprouts,
Breaking all the norms of life,
That of which I had lost grip,
Is now in blossom full, is rife!

A melody from far off land,
Plays on the strings of my soul,
As I sit in solitude, gather myself,
Agglutinate the parts, in one whole!

Eons have passed in years unknown,
Time never stood in abeyance for me,
Memoirs of my own celebrations,
Dances within my heart, in all its glee!

From hills to plains, I treaded all,
Now I swim in that distant sea,
My elan vital is on a sojourn bliss,
And am en masse, deluged within me!!

Its You In All!

In my scorching rays and in my rain,
In my smile of joy, and in my pain,
In my elevated spirit and my down soul,
In my partial me, and my complete whole,
In my beautiful life and my coming death,
In my astonished blinks and my deep breath,
In my heart's throb and my pulse's beat,
In my expanse all, and in the micro tit-bit,
In my day plain, and in celebrations grand,
In my fertile earth, and in my barren land,
In my emotions all, and my indifferences,
In my non-priorities and my preferences,
In my making of myself, and in my broken me,
In my royal giving, and in my keeping it be;

Its You that have existed in all my doings well,
And its You in my unlisted, haphazard, lost self!

A Dream!

What I have, what they seem,
Are but some alluring dream,
Everything is but a mirage well,
What you do say and what I tell;

What I hear, those sounds aerial,
What I visualize, images superficial,
Mind, a apparatus, always at work,
Lighting stories, hidden in the dark;

Standing in the shore, clasping sand,
All slides, through my feeble hand,
Much I want to hold, and clutch on,
A dream is a dream, comes to be gone!

You, Me, Silence!

A silent women, is beautiful,
As she waits for her returning love,
A silent nature, is beautiful,
As it waits for its retreating dove!

A silent brook, is beautiful,
As it rushes to meet its river bay,
A silent river is beautiful,
As it flows & meets its sea, oneday!

A silence, among two hearts,
A silence when it says perhaps the all,
That silence, I do revere,
Let, then it prevail, for us, the two souls!

I Adhere To You!

I adhere to you, for my life,
I adhere to you, because I want to survive!

I adhere to you, for my breathe,
I adhere to you, as you cool me in my seethe!

I adhere to you, like a clhild,
I adhere to you, as you are tame and am wild!

I adhere to you, fit into rough edge,
I adhere to you, surrender to you, this fact I allege!

I adhere to you, seek a support,
I adhere to you, like that ship which finds home in port!

I adhere to you, feeling, I will last forever,
I adhere to you, as I am sure that I will leave you never!

I adhere to you, as I fear a sudden storm,
I adhere to you, as you will help me realize my transform!

I adhere to you, I really know not why,
I adhere to you, and will keep on doing so, till all ends, and I die!

Have you been a lover ever?

Have you been a lover ever?
Ever cried in silence?
Ever heard the approaching footsteps,
Amongst all its absence?
Have you smiled, for reasons unknown,
Ever danced in rain?
Ever sang a forgotten song, while,
Groaning in utmost pain?
Have you waited for hours together,
Ever with a palpitated heart?
Ever vowed a thousand promises,
Of 'never shall we part'?
Have you gazed into the mirror, I ask,
Ever, sixty times in an hour?
Ever did you talk and convince yourself,
Of being a perfect lover?
Have you sighed and blabbered alone
Ever said yes 'I am in love'?
Ever blushed by remembrance random,
While gazing at the sky above?
Have you floated with the white clouds,
Ever blown in the breeze?
Ever have you felt the warmth of love,
In winter chilling freeze?

Have you felt the chill in spine, I ask you,
Ever in the june heat?
Ever felt sad and happy together,
Emotions took a back seat?

If a 'yes' adorns as an answer, to all that I ask,
Lucky you are, lover you are, sans all the mask!

Beautiful Again!

Sky melts to float on earth,
Long wait of both ends...
I watch from my window...
How the horizon and sea blends!

Monsoon dances salsa
Wearing her trinklets new...
And the branches swing...
As if they enjoy the view!

Few parrots seek shelter,
Beneath my window pane...
Few divine empyrean drops...
And oh all is beautiful again!

World In Insomniac Eyes!

Last night it was well past four,
When all surrendered to sleep;
Wrapped themselves in peace,
Behind their four walls, shut doors.

I took a virtual flight, to see you,
Across the blue hills, azure sea;
I travelled, I carried myself, for me;
And did get a glimpse of divine you.

The stars were drunk and drowsy,
The moon wore cloud's warm blanket;
Sea slept wearing the wavy locket,
Roads were lonely, dark and grumpy.

I saw you in faded caliginous light,
Some shadow fell on your face;
Am hurrying, crossing a maze,
A madness at the dead end of night.

Beautiful night, rests in your slumber,
Innocent night, in my insomniac eyes;
Sees virtues all... denounces all vice,
Tried to pretend, to get lost in you forever.

Morning tiptoed in, treading upon my dreams,
Better senses dawned, with the rising sun;
I smiled on my folly own, now noon too is done,
In twelve hours, I passed a day it seems...!

Joy Of Moving

To get the life I love,
I have packed my bag..
I got to leave..
I got to swim rivers many..
I got climb many a hill..
Many a ocean will I surf..
And be with the stars, above..
Many autumns will fall on me..
From me shall rise springs many..
Summer, winter, all shall be ..
With and always for me!
Those alluring forests ..
And enchanting brooks..
And the crimson horizon afar ..
All shall mingle into me..
As I walk alone..
On those black tar ..
Roads like curvy serpents..
Shall bend for me..
If I follow my heart..
Laid on those roads..
I will reach, maybe..
Vagabond thus sets foot out..
Alone, out of the world..
Oh, what joy it is, to move ..
Away and apart!

Traveller

Every time I leave myself behind
And take a road unknown
To go somewhere I never had been
I carry you in my heart
Deep within!
The breeze that blows my hair away
I feel it's you
The road that I walk alone
Each step, I tread with you!
I open my eyes to see
And feel you are seeing too
I travel to find myself,
My search never ends
But to find me, I get you
Strange is this ordeal!

When I travel,
A new silence
Grows within me,
And if I listen,
I do hear
What my heart
Always longed to say.

Light from you, falls on my path,
All gets illuminated
Fool I am to think to be lone
It's you, with me all the way

My journey becomes sacred one
It turns to be a pilgrimage
I go alone, with you
How can we be separate?

When you travelled without me
And smiled seeing those mountains blue
Did you not think of me even once
As much as in jungles I thought of you!

Lovers never travel alone,
They carry each other in their heart
To themselves they are always together..
To the world apart!